THE BUTCHER BAKER

THE SEARCH FOR ALASKAN SERIAL KILLER ROBERT HANSEN

REAGAN MARTIN

Absolute Crime Press
ANAHEIM, CALIFORNIA

Copyright © 2019 by Minute Help, Inc.

All rights reserved. No part of this publication may be reproduced, distributed or transmitted in any form or by any means, including photocopying, recording, or other electronic or mechanical methods, without the prior written permission of the publisher, except in the case of brief quotations embodied in critical reviews and certain other noncommercial uses permitted by copyright law.

Contents

About Absolute Crime 1
Prologue 2
Chapter One 7
Chapter Two 16
Chapter Three 32
Chapter Four 46
Chapter Five 61
Epilogue 71
Bibliography 77

About Absolute Crime

Absolute Crime publishes only the best true crime literature. Our focus is on the crimes that you've probably never heard of, but you are fascinated to read more about. With each engaging and gripping story, we try to let readers relive moments in history that some people have tried to forget.

Remember, our books are not meant for the faint at heart. We don't hold back--if a crime is bloody, we let the words splatter across the page so you can experience the crime in the most horrifying way!

If you enjoy this book, please visit our homepage (www.AbsoluteCrime.com) to see other books we offer; if you have any feedback, we'd love to hear from you!

Prologue

In 1867, when the United States purchased the territory of Alaska from the Russians at a cost of .02 cents an acre totaling 7.2 million dollars, many people wondered why they would even want it.

Despite the fact that it is the largest state in America, measuring twice the size of Texas, most people picture Alaska as little more than a vast and frozen wilderness. A desolate wasteland teeming with an array of wild animals such as grizzly bears, wolves, coyotes and moose. At the time of its acquisition, most Americans viewed it as a major waste of money.

Of course, that was before the discovery of oil. Throughout history, many people knew the state was loaded with oil. So much oil, in fact, that in some places it seeped above the ground and pooled on the surface.

In the late 1800's, minor exploration was being done, but no huge finds were discovered. It wasn't until after 1958, when Alaska gained statehood, that huge oil and gas reserves were discovered there in astounding abundance. But at the time there was little need for the precious fossil fuel, and no way to transport it from Alaska to the lower 48 states.

But in 1973, when the price of oil skyrocketed and the United States was plunged into what became known as the 'oil crisis', drilling in Alaska finally became economically feasible. Almost immediately, construction was begun on an 800-mile pipeline to be used for transporting oil from the northern part of the state to Valdez, Alaska.

Such a major construction project required massive amounts of workers, and all types of people began to flood into the state. Not just pipeline workers, but literally anyone who believed they might make a quick buck off this new industry themselves.

Some were legitimate business people, opening hotels and motels, restaurants, stores, and clubs; establishments needed to cater to the growing demand. But along with these honest folks, Alaska had its fair share of shady characters arriving as well. Everyone from prostitutes and pimps, to con men and thieves poured into the state, hoping to make some quick and lucrative cash.

Most of them were transient types, making their riches quickly, and then disappearing as fast as they had come. They had no ties to the area, no family, no friends, no one to wonder and worry about where they might be. It was not unusual for them to be here one day, and gone the next.

It was for just this reason that no one gave it a second thought when young prostitutes, and topless dancers, began vanishing around the city in the late 1970's and early 80's. Most people, including law enforcement, just assumed they had moved on to more lucrative endeavors.

Chapter One

Megan Emerick was a pretty 17-year-old girl, with chestnut brown hair, hazel eyes, and a spray of freckles across her cheeks. In the summer of 1973, Megan wasn't a prostitute or a topless dancer, but only a student at the Seward Skill Center in Seward, Alaska. She had grown up in the town, which was situated in the southern part of the state on the Kenai Peninsula.

On July 7th Megan visited the school's laundry room to wash some clothes, and spoke to several other students who were there. After a while she bid them farewell and left the building. It was the last time anyone would see Megan again.

Megan's roommate was not initially concerned when she didn't come home that night, but as the days progressed and she realized Megan had left all of her possessions, including her identification, behind, she finally contacted the police.

Although an investigation was begun, there was no sign of Megan, and no indication of foul play. The teen was simply gone, and police had no clues as to what had happened to her.

Almost exactly two years later, on July 5, 1975, 22-year-old Mary Thill disappeared as well. Mary's husband was away, working on the pipeline, while Mary remained in Seward living on Lower Point Road. She was last seen near the waterfall in town around 2:00 o'clock in the afternoon.

Mary's husband rushed back to Seward when he learned of her disappearance and helped police search for her. But no trace of Mary was ever found, and she remains missing to this day.

Police viewed the Emerick and Thill disappearances as isolated and separate incidents. Each case was investigated and worked, but as no new leads were discovered, and new cases came up, they were eventually delegated to the cold case files.

As the 1970's moved into the 1980's, Anchorage police noted an increase in the number of missing person's reports, the majority of which were for prostitutes and topless dancers. Although questions were asked, these cases were not vigorously investigated.

Police knew that ever since the pipeline had gone in and the oil industry boomed, women had been coming to the area on a daily basis. Many of the prostitutes actually worked a swing loop beginning in California, and moving up the coast to Oregon, Washington, and eventually Alaska. In each location they would stay a short time, and then move on.

Their transient lifestyles made it difficult for authorities to determine if they truly had disappeared, or simply moved on. On several occasions, police had wasted both time and energy investigating a missing persons' report, only to find the girl working the streets in another city.

It was frustrating for officers, who had neither the manpower, nor the resources to investigate all the disappearances that were reported to them. As a result, unless a body showed up, or there were clear signs of foul play involved, a missing prostitute or topless dancer was out of luck. Their name would be taken, a few inquiries made, and then the case would be shelved.

In late June of 1980, 24-year-old Roxanne Easlund, a known prostitute, was reported missing by her family. She was last seen near 4th Avenue, an area in downtown Anchorage known for its strip clubs and prostitutes, on June 28, 1980. Police took a missing persons report, and asked a few questions, but there was no indication of foul play, and the case went nowhere.

One month later, on July 21, 1980, construction workers at a job site on Eklutna Road near the Knik River made a grisly discovery. Buried in a shallow grave, near a power line, they found a jumble of decomposed and skeletonized bones.

Anchorage police cordoned off the scene and began delicately excavating the grave, placing each bone carefully within a waiting body bag. The partial remains appeared to be that of a young female, but they were badly decomposed, and what nature hadn't devoured from the body, wild animals had.

Much of the body was missing, but the skull was present, visible remnants of long, reddish-brown hair still clinging to it, and the teeth were intact. Also recovered from the grave were several pieces of jewelry, including a wristwatch, with the time stopped at a little after 11:00, a ring, an earring, a cuff bracelet and a necklace. Most of the jewelry appeared to be handmade, and possibly Native American since most of it contained turquoise stones.

Police were certain this was not the missing Roxanne Easlund. This body appeared to have been buried for a long time, a fact that the medical examiner's findings confirmed. The remains belonged to a young female in her late teens or early twenties, who was small in stature, standing only 4'11" tall, and had probably been dead about a year. The medical examiner found injuries consistent with a stabbing, and attributed her death to that.

Authorities went through their stack of missing persons' reports, and were surprised to find that none of them matched this description. They had no idea who the girl might be and turned to the public for help in identifying her. Using her skull, they created a facial reconstruction of what she might have looked like in life and released it to the media.

But no one came forward to identify the dead girl, who police had quickly dubbed 'Eklutna Annie', and with no leads to follow the case soon went cold.

In July of that same year, 23-year-old Joanne Messina went missing from the town of Seward. She was last seen leaving her job at a cannery, accompanied by her dog. Her body would be discovered later that fall, secreted within a moldy sleeping bag, in another shallow grave not far from where Eklutna Annie was found.

Joanne too was badly decomposed, and animals had carried off a good portion of her body. It was determined that she died from a

.22 caliber bullet wound, but there were few other clues to go on, and just like Eklutna Annie, Joanne Messina's case soon went cold.

Only two months after Joanne vanished, Lisa Futrell also disappeared. Lisa differed from the other girls because of her age. While those who vanished earlier had all been young, in their late teens or early twenties, Lisa might be considered middle aged at 41. Still, her background was similar enough to the other girls that law enforcement could not discount her.

In early 1981, 22-year-old Andrea Altiery, a topless dancer who worked on 4th Avenue, also disappeared. Andrea was a tough girl, who was last seen in Anchorage, wearing blue jeans, a winter coat, and her custom made fish necklace. This piece of jewelry was a priceless treasure to Andrea, and she was rarely seen without it. It was a small sterling silver charm, crafted into the shape of a fish, and always dangling from her neck.

On November 17, 1981, 24-year-old Sherry Morrow, a dancer at the Wild Cherry Bar in downtown Anchorage, told her friends that she was going to meet a man who had offered her

$300 to pose for nude photos. Sherry never returned home, and friends quickly reported her missing to the police.

Six months later, Sue Luna, a tiny 23-year-old Asian girl who had come to Alaska from Washington State, disappeared after telling friends that she was meeting a man at a downtown restaurant around noon. She walked off to keep her appointment, and that was the last time Sue Luna was ever heard from again.

# # #

If police were concerned about all these missing girls, they certainly never went public with it. Officials were aware that there were similarities among all the disappearances, but it was just such similarities that made the cases difficult to investigate. Was there foul play involved, or had the women just left on their own?

That question was impossible to answer until something showed up to point them in the right direction. Either the girl would eventually turn up in another location, or a body needed to be found before police could investigate further. Law enforcement officials were frustrated with their lack of progress, and eager for any new developments. They waited anxiously for a break, and as they did so, more women continued to disappear.

Chapter Two

John Daily and Audi Holloway, two off-duty Anchorage police officers, were spending a few much needed days off twenty-five miles north of the city in the Knik River Valley. Considered prime hunting ground for those experienced enough to brave its isolated wilderness, the valley is replete with all types of wildlife, including black bear, Dahl sheep, mountain goats, elk and moose.

On September 12, 1982, the men had hunted all day with little luck, and evening was fast approaching. Deciding to head back to camp, Daily and Holloway began walking the banks of the winding Knik River, avoiding the tangled scrub that lined each shore. Crossing a sandbar, each man noticed something sticking up from the silt and paused.

"What is that?" Holloway asked, pointing.

Daily shook his head, squinting his eyes in an effort to see it better. "I don't know."

The two men continued to walk, the object coming closer and closer, until they could distinguish that it was actually a boot jutting up from the sand. This was not that unusual, but the fact that there was a skeletonized leg bone in it was.

Backing away slowly, the men noted the location and peered around. There was nothing visible in close proximity to the boot, but they had no intention of looking any further. They were, after all, police officers, and the last thing they wanted to do was contaminate a crime scene. It was too late to try and hike out of the gorge tonight, so Daily and Holloway went back to camp and summoned help the next morning.

Sergeant Rollie Port of the Anchorage Police Department arrived on the scene early and ordered the entire area photographed. Carefully, using small trowels, he and his men excavated the grave, uncovering a badly decomposed, fully clothed skeleton. An ace bandage was tangled through remnants of curly blonde hair, indicating to investigators that the victim may have been blindfolded when she was killed.

Sergeant Port had the corpse photographed from every angle, then helped place the remains gently into a body bag. Working with large metal screens, investigators began sifting the sand from the excavated grave, finding their first clue when the screen revealed a single shell casing from a .223 caliber bullet. Port knew that this type of ammunition was used in high-powered rifles, such as M-16's, Mini-14's, or AR-15's. The shell casing was a good clue for ballistic purposes, but as far as the ammunition itself, it was not that unusual. The high powered rifles capable of firing the shell were preferred weapons of big game hunters, and the majority of the Alaskan population probably owned some type of high powered weapon.

Back in Anchorage, the medical examiner determined that the body was that of a female, who had been dead at least six months, maybe more. She had died from three gunshot wounds made by .223 caliber bullets. Interestingly, her clothing showed no signs of bullet holes or tears. Sergeant Port was intrigued by this. It appeared that the victim had been nude when her killer shot her, and had then been re-dressed before she was buried. But why?

It would take investigators a little over two weeks to determine that the dead woman found on the Knik River was 24-year-old Sherry Morrow, who had been missing since November 17, 1981. She had last told friends that she was going to meet a man who had offered her $300 to pose for some nude photos.

# # #

Finally, after the discovery of Sherry Morrow's body, Anchorage Police were willing to consider the possibility that there was someone out there murdering topless dancers and prostitutes. They knew about the increase in missing person's reports, and of course, the discovery of Eklutna Annie and Joanne Messina. Now, having found that Sherry Morrow was also a victim of murder, they were willing to concede that they might have a serial killer on their hands.

But if they were admitting this among themselves, they were reluctant to reveal it to the public. Fearing that doing so would tip off the killer, Detective Maxine Farrell told the Anchorage Daily News that she doubted the deaths of the three girls were connected. 'We don't believe we have a mass murderer out there. Some psycho knocking off girls,' she said.

But that's exactly what the prostitutes and topless dancers believed. They were convinced there was a predator out there, targeting them, preying on them, and they berated the Anchorage Police for not taking the disappearances more seriously.

The police understood their frustration, but they strongly disagreed with their assessment. They had investigated the girl's disappearances, and questioned everyone they could think of, from friends to bar owners, to pimps, to aggressive johns, in an effort to find out what had happened to them. And still, they weren't sure who was actually 'missing', and who had simply left town on their own.

But the discovery of the three murdered women and the others that were still missing had the Anchorage Police Department very concerned. They asked the Alaska State Police for assistance with the investigation, and after they joined forces, the two agencies began sharing information.

\#   \#   \#

Seven months would pass since Sherry Morrow's body was found in the lonely grave by the Knik River, and in that time, more women would continue to disappear. In April of 1983, 17-year-old Paula Golding was wondering how her life had taken such a drastic turn.

Paula had come to Alaska, like all those before her, to try and improve her financial situation, and in the beginning, things went well for the girl. She found a good job as a secretary, earning excellent money in the booming economy, secured a nice apartment, and made several new friends. But just as quickly, things had begun to fall apart on her.

She lost her secretarial job and was unable to find another, and any savings she had managed to acquire soon ran out. She needed to find work that paid well, and find it fast. But there was not much out there that fit that criteria, and reluctantly she ended up taking a job as an exotic dancer at a gentleman's club downtown.

On the evening of April 25, 1983, Paula Golding was seen near 4th Avenue, outside a strip club in the city of Anchorage. And then she vanished. Friends of the missing teen reported her disappearance to local police, but there were no leads to follow and no suspects, and as with all the other women who had disappeared, Paula's case soon went cold.

#   #   #

Less than two months later, at 5:00 am on the morning of June 13, 1983, a local truck driver was shocked to see a scantily clad woman run in front of his vehicle. The girl was screaming, and waving her arms frantically, in an effort to get him to stop. The driver screeched to a halt, and as he did so, he noticed the furtive shadow of a man slinking away between two buildings.

The woman, who was little more than a teenager, raced to the passenger side door and climbed in. She was nearly hysterical, sobbing and crying that a man was trying to get her. Dangling from her left wrist was a pair of silver, shiny handcuffs.

The distraught girl asked the driver to take her to a nearby motel, and once there, she went inside and called her pimp. But her rescuer, surprised that she seemed to have no intention of calling the police, drove directly to the police station and reported the incident.

Officer Gregg Baker arrived at the motel to find the girl alone, and still in handcuffs. He removed the cuffs, and then listened in astonishment as the girl told him her story.

She was 17-years-old, and working as a topless dancer at one of the clubs on 4th Avenue. Earlier that evening, a red-haired man who wore glasses and had a heavily pockmarked face had approached her and offered her $200 to perform oral sex on him.

The teen readily agreed, and got into the passenger side of the man's truck. But while performing the act, the man had snapped a handcuff around her wrist, and pulled a gun on her. He then cuffed both hands in front of her and drove her to a house in the Muldoon section of the city.

Once there, the man had taken her to the basement, stripped her naked, and ordered her to stand against a wooden support beam. Chaining her body to the beam, he then raised her cuffed wrists and suspended them to a hook in the ceiling. The man then spent several hours torturing her, biting her breasts, and sexually assaulting her with the handle of a hammer.

After what seemed like an eternity, her kidnapper laid down on a couch and fell fast asleep. The terrified girl knew she was in serious trouble, and searched for a way to escape. But there was no way out, so instead, she decided to take note of her surroundings, memorizing every detail in the hope that if she lived through this, she could put this sadist behind bars.

The basement walls were covered with what was obviously the trophies of an experienced and avid hunter. The mounted heads of deer, elk, moose and sheep stared back at her, their dead glass eyes fixed and unseeing. There were stuffed birds resting in a corner, and a large bear skin rug on the floor.

Looking upwards, toward her suspended hands, she took note of several long scratch marks in the beam near the hook. She memorized the layout of the furnishings, and carefully studied her attacker as he slept. He was thin, slight, and woefully unattractive, his skin so badly blemished that she would later describe him as a 'crater face.'

After several hours the man awoke and assaulted her again, then released her aching arms from the hook and stood face to face with her, staring intently.

"I like you." He said, his face so close to hers that she could actually smell his foul breath. "I like you a lot." His gaze was intense, leering. He paused, as if thinking, then continued. "I'll tell you what; I'm going to fly you up to my cabin, and if you'll have sex with me there, I'll let you go."

For a moment, the girl felt a surge of hope rise within her. But she wasn't stupid, and almost instantly she realized that if she got into this man's plane, she would never be coming back. She wanted to object, but she was afraid too. Instead, she nodded her head and whispered 'Okay.'

The two drove out to Merrill Air Field, where the man directed her over to a small, two-seater plane. Unlocking one of the handcuffs, he threw it over a small pipe running along the top of the plane, and then locked her hand back in it. She could now move the length of the pipe, but no further.

As the man returned to his truck, carrying bags back and forth to the plane, the girl worked on the handcuffs. She pulled at her hands, yanking and twisting them until the cold steel cut into her flesh, tearing her wrists and allowing blood to run freely down her arms.

And then, incredibly, her right hand slipped through the locked cuff and she was free. Amazed, she turned to see the man bending into his truck, his back towards her, his body halfway inside the vehicle. Terrified and excited, all at the same time, the girl saw her chance to escape and she took it.

She bolted from the plane, running as fast as she could, fleeing from this man she was certain would kill her. She didn't know where she was or where she was going, and she didn't care. She had to get away because the man was chasing her.

The petrified girl could hear him gaining ground behind her, his heavy boots slapping against the pavement. She had no shoes on, and she was aware of the gravelly tarmac cutting into the flesh of her feet, slowing her down, but she was oblivious to any pain.

Up ahead, almost like a miracle, the girl saw two headlights piercing the dark road. With renewed energy, she burst forth and ran into the middle of the street. She had no intention of moving. If the truck hit her, she thought, so be it. It would surely be an easier death than what her kidnapper had in mind. But the truck didn't hit her. It stopped abruptly, and her attacker scurried away.

# # #

Officer Baker was stunned by the girl's story. He transported her down to police headquarters, where she gave a formal statement. Several detectives then drove her out to Merrill Airfield where they cruised back and forth among the numerous planes. Finally, the girl shouted for the officers to stop, and pointed to a blue and white Piper Super Cub with tail #N3089Z.

Learning from the flight tower that the plane was owned by a man named Robert Hansen who lived on Old Harbor Road in the Muldoon section of the city, police dropped the teen off at the hospital and then proceeded to Hansen's home.

There, they were greeted by 40-year-old Bob Hansen, a small, thin man with red hair, glasses, and a severely pockmarked face. When they explained to the man why they were there, Hansen was incensed. He was adamant that he had never met the teen, and had certainly not abducted her. He had been out all evening, first having dinner with friends, and then playing poker with them till the wee hours of the morning.

The suspect explained that he was a happily married man with a family and a successful bakery in town. His wife and children were traveling in Europe, he said, while he stayed behind to run their business.

He seemed to want to impress upon the lawmen that he was way above consorting with prostitutes. He was well liked and respected in the community, he asserted, which was probably why the 'hooker' was telling such a ridiculous story. It seemed obvious to him that it was nothing more than an attempt to shake him down for money.

The police listened quietly as the man continued to fume. It was totally absurd, he insisted, "You can't rape a prostitute can you?" he asked sarcastically.

Police knew that you could, indeed, rape a prostitute, but they didn't bother to point this out to their suspect. They found Robert Hansen to be arrogant and pretentious, and they disliked the man immediately. But they held their tongues. The baker seemed to be cooperative, even asking if they'd like to come in and search his house.

They certainly would, the officers said. Making their way to the basement, the detectives were surprised to see that very little matched what the teen had told them. While it was furnished as the girl described, there were no animal heads mounted on the walls, no stuffed birds staring from the corner recesses, and no bear skin rug on the floor. They used flashlight to look above the beam they assumed was the one the girl was chained to, but they found no hook screwed into the ceiling, and no scratches as she had described.

Thanking Bob Hansen for his help, the police next paid a visit to his two alibi witnesses. The two men corroborated what Hansen had told them, agreeing that he had been with them all evening.

The Anchorage police were puzzled. The young prostitute had seemed so credible, so undeniably terrified and in shock, but now they were beginning to wonder. Could Bob Hansen be telling the truth? Could this girl be making the whole story up in an effort to extort money from him?

Wanting to be sure, they asked the girl if she would be willing to take a polygraph, and when she refused, their doubts increased. As bad as that was, it would actually be the medical findings that would sink the girl's case. Doctors reported finding no signs of bruising or tearing of her genitals, no semen, and no indication of rape at all.

With no physical evidence against Bob Hansen, and two respected businessmen willing to give him an alibi, the case came down to the word of a 17-year-old prostitute against that of a well respected, married father. For the District Attorney, it was a no-brainer on who would win that one, and he quickly declined to press charges.

Chapter Three

While some police officers chose to believe that the young prostitute was lying about being kidnapped by Bob Hansen, there were others who weren't so sure. State Trooper Glenn Flothe was one of them. He believed the girl's story, and was determined to keep an eye on Bob Hansen.

Less than two months after the young girl's kidnapping, on September 2, 1983, the body of 17-year-old Paula Golding was found buried in a shallow grave near the Knik River. The proximity of the remains, so close to the other murdered women, and the fact that police found an ace bandage and the casing from a .223 caliber bullet in the grave, finally convinced them that they were dealing with only one killer.

Only a week later, 20-year-old DeLynn Frey was reported missing. Frey had not been seen since March, so could have vanished anytime between then and September. No one was really sure when she had gone missing, nor could they recall where she might have been going when she disappeared.

Trooper Glenn Flothe was disheartened by the news that another girl had vanished, and he thought often about the young prostitute who had accused the Anchorage baker of kidnapping her. Although it had been nearly three months since he last saw Bob Hansen, Flothe had not forgotten him. Just who was Bob Hansen, the detective wondered?

# # #

Robert Christian Hansen was born on February 15, 1939, in Esterville, Iowa, the only child of Christian and Edna Hansen, an extremely religious couple. His father was a strict disciplinarian, and his mother seemed to acquiesce to anything her husband suggested.

Christian Hansen was mortified to see that his son had been born left-handed, a condition he considered a defect, and he and his wife forced the little boy to use his right hand for everything, demanding that Bob sit on his left hand while he wrote or ate.

When Bob was still small, the family moved to California, but returned to Iowa when he turned 10. There his father opened his own bakery, and ordered his son to work in it daily. The little boy would be there before school and after, working long hours for a salary of $1.00 a day.

By the time Bob reached the age of 12 he was considered a loner in his school with few friends. This was not by choice, but due to the fact that Bob portrayed the image of the All-American 'nerd'. The boy had a severe speech impediment, stuttering wildly whenever he spoke, and he was small, with bright red hair and large framed glasses. Worse yet, he had a severe case of acne that covered his entire face. He was teased mercilessly by both boys and girls, and continuously referred to as 'zit face', 'pizza face', and 'pimple puss.'

Bob was under a lot of stress at school because of this, and felt just as much anxiety at home. His parents were constantly yelling at him at work, and the pressure he felt whenever they berated him for using his left hand greatly exacerbated his speech impediment. He took to dealing with his stress by picking at his pimply face, tearing open the sores that would later heal into deep, indented scars.

Bob wanted to fit in, he just never seemed able too. His heavy workload at the bakery kept him from socializing with his peers or making new friends. At the age of 14 he tried out for the school's basketball team and was thrilled when he made it. But he was greatly disappointed to spend most of his time warming the bench. He did much better on the track team, competing in long distance running and the broad jump, two areas he earned a letter in. But neither of these accomplishments helped to endear him to his fellow students.

After a while, Bob quit trying to fit in, instead spending all his free time alone, pursuing solitary activities. He loved to hunt and fish, and became skilled at archery. To most of the kids he went to school with, Bob was a loser.

In 1957, at the age of 18 he was ready to graduate, but not before his high school sent him away with one last humiliation. Leafing through his yearbook, he noted with embarrassment that they had spelled his name wrong.

Bob wasn't sure what he wanted to do with his life but he was anxious to try something other than the bakery. He joined the Army Reserve and was sent to Fort Dix, New Jersey to complete his basic training. Here, Bob seemed to break free. He had never had a girlfriend, not even a date, but now, while visiting Fort Know Kentucky, he threw caution to the wind and picked up a prostitute. Bob was a virgin, and the two of them had sex in a motel room, the more experienced woman telling him what to do. After that, Bob discovered that he liked sex, and he continued to visit prostitutes on a regular basis.

In 1959, at the age of 20, Bob was relieved from his service and returned to Iowa. He immediately went back to work with his father at the bakery, but he remained in the Army Reserves military police, fulfilling his obligation one weekend a month. He volunteered to become a drill instructor for the junior police, and enjoyed working with the youngsters.

During this time Bob met a much younger girl and the two began dating. In 1960, after just turning 21, the couple married and settled into a rental house not far from his father's bakery. Bob became active in the local fire company and signed up as a volunteer fireman around the same time.

On December 7, 1960, a fire broke out at a school bus garage in Pocahontas Iowa, and Bob was one of the firemen responding to the scene. Unbeknownst to his fellow firefighters, he was also the one who started the blaze. Bob had convinced a 16-year-old fellow worker at the bakery to join him in this endeavor, explaining to the kid that it was 'retribution' for what he called 'perceived abuses' by the townspeople.

It was a stupid thing for him to do, as the youth soon cracked and confessed everything.

Bob Hansen was quickly arrested, charged and convicted of arson.

Sentenced to three years in prison, he was released after only 20 months and returned home to find that his wife had divorced him, and he had deeply shamed his parents. His father refused to allow him to work in the bakery any longer, and the young man drifted aimlessly, taking on one low-paying job after another.

In 1963, when he was twenty-four-years old, Bob met a pretty young lady named Darla and the two fell in love. In the fall of that same year they were married in a small ceremony and attempted to settle down and start their life together.

Although from outward appearances things seemed to be improving for Bob, it was not all peaches and cream for the young couple. Several times over the next few years, Bob would be caught stealing and shoplifting, although he was never charged with these crimes.

His arson conviction made life difficult for him in the small town. It had ruined his reputation, and labeled him as untrustworthy, and he had not been able to secure a decent job since his release from prison. He was still on the outs with his parents, and he spoke often of moving away and starting over. In the summer of 1967 he finally convinced his wife to do so.

The Hansens chose Alaska as their new destination, in part because the state gives its residents special benefits to live there, but mainly because it was the optimum terrain for an avid hunter. The two were excited by the move, and purchased a house in the middle-class section of Muldoon, just outside of Anchorage. They were anxious to begin anew, and hopefully start a family.

In Anchorage, Bob's past was completely unknown, and his dream of starting over was within easy grasp. He got along well with his fellow citizens, and became known as an avid outdoorsman and a skilled shot with the rifle. For three years in a row, 1969, 1970, and 1971 he had four animals entered into the Pope & Young Trophy Hunting World Record Book. He gained much attention one year when he brought down a Dahl sheep with his bow and arrow.

Things seemed to be going well for the Hansen's up until 1977 when Bob was arrested for stealing a chainsaw. Sentenced to five years in prison, he underwent psychiatric testing and was diagnosed as having bipolar defective disorder. Doctors prescribed a Lithium program to control his mood swings, and ordered him to remain on it even after his release. Bob served only one year of his five year sentence, and immediately quit taking his medication when he left prison. He returned home to his wife, who had stuck by him this time, and their two children.

In the early 1980's, Bob reported that someone had broken into his house and stole several of his hunting trophies, along with jewelry and electronics. The break-in netted him $13,000 in insurance claim money, and he used this to buy his own bakery in downtown Anchorage.

His business quickly flourished, becoming so successful that in January of 1982, Bob purchased his own airplane. Curiously though, he never bothered to get his pilot's license. He was regarded as a well-respected member of the community, the type of guy who eagerly volunteered his time if it was needed, and regularly attended church with his family each Sunday. From all appearances, the Hansens of Anchorage, Alaska were living the good life.

#   #   #

Although Trooper Flothe was willing to concede that there were some shady spots in Bob Hansen's background, he still wasn't convinced that the baker was the killer he hunted. It seemed unbelievable that a successful married man, the father of two small children, could be a sadistic serial killer. And yet, there were several things about Bob Hansen that fit.

For one thing, he was an avid hunter and an expert shot. The .223 caliber bullets found with the dead girls had been fired from a high-powered rifle, just the sort of weapon Hansen was bound to own. Even more intriguing was the fact that Hansen was familiar with the area where the bodies were discovered.

While interviewing a neighbor of Bob's, the man told police that he and Bob often hunted out near the Knik River, adding that it was 'one of Bob's favorite spots.' Hansen was a trophy hunter, the man explained, and always looking for the next bigger, better, more challenging kill. 'That's what trophy hunters do', the man said.

This conversation led Flothe and others to wonder if the missing women were 'trophies' to Bob Hansen. As truly frightening as the thought might be, did the killer, after having flown his victims out to the Knik River, strip them, blindfold them, and then turn them loose in the wilderness? Did he then stalk them like wild game, hunting them down and killing them like he would a deer or a bear? As insane a thought as it was, law enforcement had to admit that the scenario tallied perfectly with the evidence.

Serial killers were a relatively new breed at the time, and even though Anchorage police and the Alaska state troopers kept returning to Bob Hansen as the most likely suspect in their case, they were still uncertain. Could such a brutal killer really function so well in society, they wondered? And although they believed that the four recovered bodies were linked, did that mean that all the missing women would be linked to them too?

Using a chart, law enforcement decided to assess what they knew so far. The city of Anchorage had a total of 17 missing girls, four of whom were found dead. All of the women had disappeared from Anchorage, with the exception of Mary Thill and Megan Emerick, who had both vanished from Seward. They were two of the thirteen women still unaccounted for. The others still missing were:

Roxanne Easlund, Lisa Futrell, Andrea Altiery, Sue Luna, Malai Larsen, DeLynn Frey, Teresa Watson, Angela Feddern, Tamara Pederson, Kathy Disher, and Karen Baumsgaurd.

Most of these 17 girls had similar backgrounds. One worked in a massage parlor, one had been arrested for prostitution in the past, and the majority of the others worked as topless dancers in the bars and clubs on 4th Avenue.

This was true for all the girls, with the exception of Megan Emerick, Mary Thill, and Joanne Messina. Curiously, none of these early victims appeared to have ties to prostitution or the bars and clubs on 4th Avenue. Police believed this difference in victims was nothing more than a matter of convenience for their killer. He probably preferred 'nice girls', but might have quickly changed his preference when he realized that prostitutes and topless dancers made far easier targets.

As police studied the disappearances, they found another similarity in what the missing women were known to have said just before they vanished. Five of them told friends and acquaintances that they were meeting a man in a downtown restaurant around noon. One claimed she was meeting a man to pose for nude photos, and another that she had been offered $300 for one hour of her time. Sherry Morrow, who was the third victim found, had told friends that she was offered $300 to pose for nude photos just before she disappeared.

Flothe thought a lot about what the women had said. What kind of man, he wondered, was available regularly at the noon hour? A typical lunch hour wouldn't provide enough time to abduct and kill someone. Perhaps he was unemployed, or even retired. Or could he be someone who owned his own business and was able to get free time off whenever he wanted? Someone whose business might allow him to do a lot of his work at night? Someone like a baker who owned his own bakery in downtown Anchorage? Flothe knew that bakers often worked the night shift, and surely, if you owned the business, you could come and go as you pleased.

As much as Bob Hansen might seem like a prime suspect, authorities knew they had another major problem. If Bob Hansen was the killer they sought, how could they prove it? They had no evidence against the man, no hair, no fibers, no DNA, nothing. Not even enough to scrounge up a search warrant for his house and plane.

What officers needed was a break, and in the hopes of finally getting one, they decided to turn to the experts for help. In mid-September of 1983, Alaska authorities placed a call to FBI headquarters in Quantico, Virginia, and asked for assistance.

Chapter Four

When the Alaska State Police contacted FBI headquarters, they were referred to the Behavioral Science unit and assigned to work with two of the best know criminal profilers in history; Roy Hazelwood and John Douglas.

As authorities from Alaska began to explain the developments that led to their suspect in the case, the FBI agents immediately cut them off.

"First tell me about the crimes," John Douglas said, "and then I'll tell you about the guy,"

State troopers described for the profiler their missing women, the details of their disappearances, the evidence recovered from the gravesites, and the story of the young girl who was kidnapped and escaped. Deliberately, and at the agent's request, they left Bob Hansen's name, and any of his details, out of the story.

After listening to the state troopers, the FBI agents went on to amaze them by describing the type of person their killer would most likely be. A man of low self-esteem, they said, unattractive, who had probably been teased and ridiculed as a child. He would have a criminal background, but probably for only petty crimes, and might have served time in jail. He would have been unsuccessful with women, would be an avid hunter, and probably suffered from a speech impediment.

Alaskan authorities were speechless. Incredibly, the profiler's had just described Robert Hansen to a T. But as remarkable as the FBI profile was in fitting their suspect, state troopers were still concerned. What about Hansen's standing in the community, they asked, the fact that he had a wife and children, his success at business? Did the FBI agents really think that this was the type of man who could be responsible for these murders?

Indeed he could be, the agents replied. But, they warned, having studied similar criminal cases, they knew that this type of killer was extremely hard to stop. Without a confession, they would probably never catch him.

The State Troopers asked John Douglas if he would come to Alaska to help them build a case against their suspect. Douglas hesitated for moment. Typically, he worked from a crime scene, attempting to determine the background and personality of a likely suspect. In this case, authorities were asking him to work with a likely suspect and try to determine if his background and personality fit the crimes. No FBI profiler had ever done such a thing before. It was so unusual, so bizarre, and so challenging, that Douglas couldn't resist. He accepted, and he and fellow agent Jim Horn quickly made arrangements to travel to Alaska.

As the two FBI men studied what was known about Bob Hansen, they began to form a picture of the man and his habits in their mind. Douglas believed that Hansen's crimes were a work in progress. He was angry at women, and had probably killed the early victims and buried their bodies in shallow graves. Eventually though, as the killings increased, he would have realized that he 'could combine the pleasure of the hunt with the kill'. Like their Alaskan counterparts, Douglas and Horn also believed that Hansen had flown these women to the remote wilderness alive, blindfolded them, possibly handcuffed them, and then set them loose, hunting them down and killing them. He had apparently gotten bored with bear and moose, and like his neighbor said, needed a bigger, better and more challenging 'game' to hunt.

Douglas also believed that Hansen's hunting rifle, the weapon he used to murder these young girls, would be extremely important to him. He would not have disposed of it, Douglas reasoned, but would probably keep it within easy reach. Hidden, of course, but most likely somewhere in his home or on his property.

They should also look for 'souvenirs', he told the Alaskan authorities. Hansen was a trophy hunter, and would be the type to take a 'trophy' from each of his kills. They should look for small items of no real value; jewelry, pictures, charms, trinkets or identification. From his experience, Douglas added, Hansen was also the type who might have kept a diary or a journal of his killings, so they should look for something like that as well.

State Troopers wanted to use the FBI profile to secure a search warrant for Bob Hansen's home and property, but this was something that had never been attempted before. The FBI was more than willing to summarize their findings in an affidavit, but they weren't sure if it would be enough. Douglas urged the Alaskan authorities to work on Hansen's alibi for the night of the kidnapping. If they could break his alibi, they'd have enough probable cause to get a search warrant.

Returning to the two men who had vouched that Bob was having dinner with them and playing poker on the night of June 13th, trooper Glenn Flothe listened as both reiterated his alibi once again. The trooper was convinced the men were lying, and he was done playing games with them. He threatened both of them with arrest, and a long prison sentence, if he discovered they were lying.

Now frightened, the two men immediately changed their stories. They had not been with Bob that evening, they explained, nor had they seen him. They had agreed to cover for him because they believed his story about the prostitute trying to extort money from him. They told officers that Hansen had described the dilemma as an 'awkward situation.'

The alibi witnesses, now anxious to remain in the good graces of Alaskan State Troopers, also blurted out something else about Bob Hansen. The break-in at his house, where he had collected $13,000 in insurance money, had been staged. Hansen had all the items he claimed were stolen, the trophies, the jewelry, and the electronics, stored in the basement of his house.

Now, armed with the FBI's profile and Bob Hansen's lack of an alibi for the night the prostitute was abducted, state trooper Glenn Flothe went before Judge Victor Carlson with a 48-page affidavit. He detailed the probable cause he believed they had to search Hansen's home and property, and Judge Carlson agreed. Authorities now had their long desired search warrant, and the excitement in the air was electrifying.

But the exhilaration was tempered with worry too. They knew that if they did not find anything, and could not break their suspect, their case was doomed.

# # #

On the morning of October 27, 1983, a detail of state troopers and Anchorage police officers arrived at the home of Bob and Darla Hansen on Old Harbor Road. Miles away, at Merrill Air Field, another group was serving a warrant to search Hansen's plane. At the same time, in downtown Anchorage, two additional vehicles, loaded with law enforcement officials, were arriving at Hansen's bakery.

This last group had followed Bob to work, and as soon as he exited his car, they asked him to accompany them back to police headquarters to answer some questions. The officers noted with interest that their suspect didn't even inquire as to what they wanted to question him about.

Back at the Hansen house, investigators were going over the premises with a fine tooth comb. They looked in closets, drawers, cupboards and dressers. They pulled books off of shelves and went through them page by page. They tapped walls, and searched for loose floorboards. They took cushions off the furniture and reached their hands deep inside the frames. They meticulously vacuumed every rug and carpet.

Every square inch of the house, every single nook and cranny they could possibly find, they searched. And they found absolutely nothing that could connect Bob Hansen to the murders.

At police headquarters, Bob sat calmly in a chair, still not asking officers why they had brought him in. He didn't appear scared, frightened, or even nervous. Instead, the arrogance that he had previously shown remained intact.

He staunchly denied having kidnapped the young prostitute, and was even more adamant that he had no involvement in the murders of the missing women. He seemed outraged, indignant, and absolutely infuriated.

Back at the house on Old Harbor Road, police had been searching all day. They had found numerous weapons, but none that could be tied to any of the killings. They had searched the house, the attic, the basement and the yard.

They had found the items that Hansen had listed as being stolen hidden in his cellar, exactly where his alibi witnesses said they would be.

"Well," one of the troopers said dejectedly, "at least we can get him on [insurance] fraud charges."

The others nodded in agreement, but each knew that charge wouldn't keep Hansen off the streets for long.

"Something's got to be here." Flothe said, unable to admit defeat.

Several others shook their heads. "We tried." One of them said, "But there's nothing here. The place is clean."

"No!" Flothe shouted, his frustration mounting. He knew something was here, he could almost smell it. "Let's check the attic one more time," he said, "let's rip out every inch of insulation up there."

Some of the investigators groaned. They had already searched the attic, they protested, there was nothing up there. But they hadn't ripped up the insulation, only poked around in it to see if anything might be hidden below. Most of them wanted to call it a day. They had been here for hours, and they were depressed that they had found nothing.

But home would have to wait. They knew they could not leave until they completed this final task.

#   #   #

Bob Hansen was pretending to be cooperative with the detectives, but his attitude was so smug that the officers had to control themselves from wiping the smirk off his face. For every piece of evidence they threw at him, he had an explanation, or a denial. The cops were frustrated and angry, and getting nowhere.

After hours and hours of interrogation, Bob Hansen could sense the officer's agitation. He was disgusted with the entire thing himself. When they relayed back to their suspect that investigators had found the missing items he had reported stolen, Bob Hansen grinned.

"Oh, that's right," he said. "You know, one day they showed up in my back yard." He shrugged. "I guess I just forgot to report it." He smiled, tilted his head, and said casually, "I think I'd like to speak to an attorney now."

'That lousy son of bitch', one of the detectives said as he exited the room, 'I swear to God, if I thought I could get away with it I'd strangle him right now'. But since they couldn't do that, much as they all might have liked too, they instead placed Bob Hansen under arrest and charged him with assault, kidnapping, weapons violations, theft, and insurance fraud. Officers placed him in a cell and left him to himself.

Back at his house, up in the attic, there were several other law enforcement officials who would have liked to strangle Bob Hansen as well. The men had pulled up nearly 90% of the fiberglass insulation from the floor rafters, and had found nothing. Their arms were scratched and pricked, and they itched like mad all over their exposed skin. Despite it being October, it was sweltering hot in the attic, and the sweat was pouring down their faces, trickling along their backs, and making the itching that much more intense.

They had but one more section of floor rafter to search, and this one was going to be a bitch. It was the section just below the roof eave of the house, in a narrow and tightly confined space. There was no way to reach it except to lie flat on your stomach and wriggle your way back there. As one of the state troopers lay down and began inching towards it, he cursed Bob Hansen up one side and down the other.

The investigator reached his hand into the insulation, and began pulling it up. It wasn't a sheet of insulation, it came out in tufts. Flinging each tuft to the side, he continued making his way further back. His hands and arms were burning from the fiberglass, and his anger mounted with each inch he took. This was ridiculous, he thought, there was nothing here.

But even as he told himself this, with his hand plunged deep inside the insulation, his fingers were brushing something foreign. For a moment, the sweat running down his back seemed to freeze and crystallize. If they were to find anything hidden within the insulation, they expected it to be a gun, but whatever he was feeling now was not a weapon. Instead, it appeared to be some sort of coarse fabric. Gently, the detective pulled it out.

It was a white canvas bag, cinched together at the top with white nylon cord. Still lying on his stomach, he maneuvered his arm around as best he could, and held it out behind him. Immediately, someone took it from his hand. Resuming his work, the trooper plunged his hand back into the insulation and instantly felt the cold stock of a gun. At that moment, he knew they had hit the jackpot.

Hidden beneath the insulation in the attic rafters of Bob Hansen's house police found a Remington .552 rifle, a Winchester 12- gauge shotgun, a Thompson contender 7-mm single-shot pistol, and last but not least, a .223 caliber Mini-14 rifle, the exact sort of weapon that had killed most of the dead girls.

The investigators were exuberant, and they clapped and cheered as the state trooper handed back each weapon he retrieved. All of the officers had the same thought in mind. We got him.

# # #

Back at headquarters, when police finally opened the white canvas bag, they were even more excited than they had been at the discovery of the weapons. Inside, they found jewelry, newspaper clippings detailing the disappearances and murders, identification cards bearing several of the missing and dead girl's names, photographs, and a carefully folded aviation map.

When officer's opened the map, they were startled to see that it was highlighted with many, many red X's. Several of the red marks corresponded to where the bodies had been found.

"My God." Glenn Flothe whispered, immediately remembering what John Douglas had said about some killers keeping a journal of their crimes. This wasn't a diary, but studying the map, Flothe realized that it might be even better. The map appeared to be a guide to the murdered girl's graves.

"Look at this." One of the officers said to Flothe, dangling a thin silver chain in front of him. Flothe stared at the necklace, a small silver charm, shaped like a fish, twirling gently before his eyes. He had heard a lot about this piece of jewelry, had even seen pictures of it. It was Andrea Altiery's custom-made fish necklace. Andrea had been missing for two years now, and her most prized possession had just been found in Robert Hansen's attic.

CHAPTER FIVE

While Robert Hansen languished in a jail cell, District Attorney Victor Krumm decided not to charge the baker with murder just yet. He wanted to wait until he had the results from the ballistic tests being done on the suspected killer's weapons. But Krumm did take what he had before the grand jury, and on November 3, 1983 they indicted Hansen on four counts; first degree assault and kidnapping, second degree theft, insurance fraud, and five counts of weapons violations. Hansen pled not guilty on all charges, and bail was set at $500,000.

No one came forward to bail the baker out, especially not his wife. Darla Hansen was living a virtual nightmare. She was stunned by her husband's arrest, and even more so by the accusations that were being levied against him. She knew Bob had his problems, but she had no clue that he might be capable of the violence police were suggesting he had committed.

Now Darla felt like the entire city of Anchorage was blaming her too, whispering about her, staring and pointing. She was ashamed and embarrassed, and she ached for her children, who were being harassed and teased by the other kids at school. She avoided going out in public as much as possible, instead choosing to remain indoors, where she mourned her troubles and cursed her husband.

Meanwhile, all of Hansen's weapons had been sent to the FBI crime lab in Washington DC, and on November 20th, they notified Alaska State Troopers that all of the shell casings found at the gravesites had been fired from Bob's .223 Mini-14 rifle. There was no doubt now that Alaska had the serial killer they had been hunting for years.

The evidence against Robert Hansen was overwhelming, and both he and his attorney,

Fred Dewey, knew it. Dewey told his client that prosecutors had more than enough evidence to convict him, and in all likelihood he would be convicted. In order to spare his wife and children any more pain and publicity, Bob Hansen reluctantly agreed to plead guilty.

On February 18, 1984, the admitted serial killer stood before Judge Ralph E. Moody and pled guilty to the murders or Eklutna Annie, Joanne Messina, Sherry Morrow, and Paula Golding. Judge Moody set a sentencing date for one week later.

Both Hansen and his attorney knew that this was just the beginning of the former baker's legal troubles. The police had evidence implicating Bob in many of the other disappearances, and a suspected map that might lead them to their graves. New charges were bound to be filed against him, and if authorities discovered other bodies, even more charges after that. Bob Hansen, and his family, could be in the headlines for years and years to come. Dewey suggested that they try to work out a deal with the D.A., and Hansen reluctantly agreed.

On February 22, 1984, Robert Hansen signed a plea agreement before his attorney and District Attorney Victor Krumm. In exchange for a full confession, the D.A. promised Bob he would only be charged with the four cases he already pled guilty too. In addition, he would allow him to serve his time in a federal penitentiary rather than state prison. Hansen had insisted on this last part because he was worried about doing time in the state penitentiary. From his past experiences in jail, Bob knew that women killers are not viewed kindly by the inmate hierarchy, and if he were sent to the state pen, he would probably serve some very hard time.

Once all parties had agreed to the deal and signed the plea agreement, Robert Hansen, in chilling detail, began confessing to his crimes. He started out by insisting that he only visited prostitutes because there were some sexual pleasures he enjoyed, but didn't feel he could ask his wife to perform. His disgust for the prostitutes was evident, while the implication that Darla was a 'good' girl, and the street whores were 'dirty', was clearly expressed.

Bob enjoyed picking up these girls, but he was loath to pay them for their services. Sometimes, he would simply rape the women, and if they cooperated fully, he would let them go. If they didn't, well... Here he simply let the sentence trail off.

He typically took the same course of action every time he got a girl into his vehicle. His first goal was to try and gain control, and often he would begin by grabbing the girls by the hair, pulling their heads back, and shoving a gun in their face. He needed to terrify them immediately, he explained, in order to insure their cooperation.

While still holding the barrel of the gun pressed against their face, Hansen said he would then proceed to give them a little speech.

'Look, you work in a dangerous profession', he would say, 'you know there's some risk to what you do. If you cooperate, and do exactly as I say, I won't hurt you.' He told the girls they should consider this a learning experience, and be more careful about who they went with next time.

He admitted that sometimes he would take them to his house first, if Darla wasn't around and he had the opportunity, but more often than not he would drive directly to Merrill Field. There, he would fly the abducted women out to his remote cabin by the Knik River, and brutally rape and torture them until he had his fill.

Confirming what investigators had long suspected, Hansen went on to say that afterwards, he would strip them, sometimes blindfold them, sometimes handcuff them, and then set them free in the wilderness. He always allowed them a little time to get a head start, and then he would begin the hunt.

With little emotion, and a deadpan voice, he told those listening how he would then stalk the girls, hunting them, tracking them, until he found them and killed them. It was just like going after a 'trophy Dahl sheep, or a grizzly bear', he said.

The police were horrified, but silent, as they listened to the repulsive killer's admissions. They couldn't begin to imagine the absolute terror these poor girls had felt while they were being hunted and stalked like wild game. The investigators deeply regretted that Bob Hansen wasn't eligible for the death penalty.

# # #

Although Hansen and his attorney had feared that the aviation map would easily lead police to the other buried bodies, they need not have. Authorities knew it would be almost impossible to pinpoint any graves just from the markings on the map. So, on February 23, 1984, they took Robert Hansen up in a military helicopter and had him direct them to the spots where he had buried his victims.

At his direction, they flew out towards the Knik River, not far from where Paula Golding and Sherry Morrow had been found. The ground was completely frozen, and covered with a deep layer of snow. Investigators knew that any remains Hansen might point out now could not be recovered until spring. They would have to come back later to begin excavating the graves. But they marked each spot with an orange stake, and took the additional precaution of using orange spray paint to mark any nearby trees.

They then flew on to Jim Creek, in the Matanuska-Susitna area, and then veered the helicopter south, down towards Horseshoe, and Figure Eight Lakes. By the end of the day, Robert Hansen had revealed the gravesites of 12 unknown victims. None were recovered that day, and it would be months before investigators knew whether the serial killer was telling the truth.

# # #

On February 27, 1984, Robert Christian Hansen stood before Judge Ralph E. Moody to receive his punishment. Judge Moody sentenced Hansen to 461 years in prison, plus life without parole. Days later, the convicted killer was taken to the Anchorage International Airport and flown thousands of miles from his home. His plane touched down in the state of Pennsylvania, and he was driven directly to the Lewisburg Federal Penitentiary to begin serving his time.

Two months later, when spring arrived in Alaska, authorities began the grim task of trying to locate the remains of Robert Hansen's victims. On April 24, they recovered the body of Sue Luna, near the Knik River, and Malai Larsen in the parking area near the old Knik Bridge.

The next day they found DeLynn Frey, who was buried near Horseshoe Lake, and the following day, the body of Angela Feddern near Figure Eight Lake, and Teresa Watson, buried on the Kenai Peninsula.

Three days later, on April 29, 1984, they located the remains of Tamara Pederson one and a half miles from the old Knik Bridge.

The search was slow, tedious, and extremely difficult. In many of the locations that Hansen had pointed out, officers found nothing at all. But they didn't think the killer was lying. It was more likely that wild animals had discovered the remains and carried them away.

But police refused to give up, and their persistence finally paid off on May 9th, when they discovered the body of Lisa Futrell buried in a shallow grave just south of the old Knik Bridge.

Of the twelve graves Bob Hansen led investigators to, police had recovered seven bodies. Eventually, they would find two more, Andrea Altiery, whose fish necklace had been found in

Hansen's attic, and a young female whose identity police were not able to discern. Four of the seventeen women Hansen is suspected of killing have never been found. They are:

    Roxanne Easlund

    Mary Thill

    Megan Emerick, and

    Celia, 'Beth' Van Zarten

Despite the fact that police could not find these last four suspected victims, they felt fortunate to have recovered as many bodies as they had. For they knew only too well that most corpses, be they animal or human, did not last long in the Alaskan wilderness.

Epilogue

For two years after his conviction, Bob Hansen's wife and children struggled to remain in Alaska, the state they considered their home. But the continual harassment never ceased, and in 1986, Darla Hansen divorced her husband and moved her family to the lower 48 states.

In 1988, Robert Hansen was returned to the state of Alaska and incarcerated as one of the first inmates at the brand new Spring Creek Correctional Center in Seward. He remains there today.

The record keepers at Pope & Young initially stated that Hansen's conviction as a serial killer had nothing to do with his world record wins in trophy hunting. But after numerous complaints, and outrage from other hunters, they soon removed his name from their record books.

Eklutna Annie has never been identified, and on February 21, 2003, Alaska State Troopers once again asked the public for help in identifying her. They described her as a white brunette, with a possible mixture of American Indian or Asian heritage, aged somewhere in her early to mid-twenties. For the first time, they also released pictures of the jewelry found with the body, in the hopes that someone might recognize it. No one did. Her burial was paid for by the state of Alaska, and she is interred at the Anchorage Memorial Cemetery, where a small bronze plaque marks her grave.

Hansen told investigators that Eklutna Annie was his first victim, but he did not know or couldn't remember her name. She was either a topless dancer or a prostitute, he said. He had abducted her with the intention of bringing her back to his house, but on the way the girl had tried to escape and in a panic he had killed her.

He thought the woman had mentioned that her family lived in Kodiak, but he couldn't be sure.

Alaskan authorities are still trying to identify Eklutna Annie, and would welcome any information about her or her identity from the general public. It is their belief that she might have come to Alaska from either Washington or California.

While confessing to the murders, Robert Hansen also admitted to raping at least 30 other Alaskan women who he did not kill. Most of these assaults were never even reported. How many girls Hansen actually killed remains a mystery. He is officially attributed with 17 murders, but some estimates put it as high as 37.

There are three marks on Hansen's aviation map, near the deep, icy waters of Resurrection Bay, two of which police believe are the gravesites of Megan Emerick and Mary Thill. Despite the fact that Hansen was in Seward on both of the days that Megan Emerick and Mary Hill vanished, he has denied any involvement in their disappearances. He has also refused to admit that these three markings near Resurrection Bay are burial sites.

Police, however, do not believe him. It is their opinion that these were Hansen's first kills, and his preferred type of victim. But Bob Hansen was no Ted Bundy who could charm beautiful college co-eds into his vehicle. He was ugly, nerdy, and sounded like the stuttering cartoon character, Porky Pig, whenever he spoke. It seems unlikely that any young females, other than those looking to make money off of him, would have accompanied him willingly.

State Trooper Glenn Flothe would later say, "He tried to make us think that he had some kind of moral code. But the reality was that these street girls and the girls in the bars were easier victims."

What propelled Bob Hansen to become a horrific serial killer remains a mystery, but many people believe it began with a short story published way back in 1924. At that time, Richard Connell wrote a book entitled The Most Dangerous Game. The story was about a big-game hunter named General Zaroff, who owned an uninhabited island surrounded by jagged and dangerous rocks. Instead of marking these rocks to warn passing ships, Zaroff was content to let the vessels plow into them, damaging their hulls, and sinking them to the bottom of the freezing depths.

General Zaroff welcomed these shipwrecked souls to his island because he had become bored with hunting tigers and leopards and elephants. Just as a drug addict constantly needs a bigger and better high to sustain his addiction, Zaroff needed a more intelligent and challenging animal to hunt. And, just like Bob Hansen, General Zaroff would let these castaways loose on his island, then stalk them, track them, and hunt them down to kill them.

It seems almost certain that Richard Connell's book influenced Bob Hansen in some way, but whether the Alaskan serial killer even knew about the story is unknown. He never claimed to have read it or been influenced by it. Still, the similarities between it and his own crimes are uncanny.

Those women that Bob Hansen so brutally murdered and tossed away like trash had families and friends who loved them and cared about them. They had their entire lives ahead of them; their hopes and dreams and fears and loves, and all of them were cut short by the brutal actions of Robert Hansen. For those girls whose bodies were recovered, they were returned to their families and given proper burials. But for the families of Roxanne Easlund, Mary Thill, Megan Emerick, and Celia 'Beth' Van Zarten, the wait is not yet over.

There is nothing more terrible for the families of murder victims, and the law enforcement officials who hunt their killers, than not having closure. Perhaps someday the great Alaskan wilderness will choose to give up more bodies, and reveal other evil secrets, hidden beneath the frozen ground.

BIBLIOGRAPHY

http://www.trutv.com/library/crime/serial_killers/weird/robert_hansen/7.html

http://www.skcentral.com/articles.php?article_id=110

http://www.criminiedelitti.com/2012/10/18/robert-christian-hansen-the-alaska-killer/

http://www.explorenorth.com/

http://www.charleyproject.org/cases/e/emerick_megan.html

http://www.nampn.org/cases/thill_mary.html

http://www.alaskahistoricalsociety.org/index.cfm/discover-alaska/FAQS/11

http://voices.yahoo.com/hunting-humans-shocking-crimes-robert.hansen-6624364.html?cat=72

http://www.murderpedia.org/male.H/hansen-robert-victims.htm

http://www.doenetwork.org/cases/311ufak.html

http://maamodt.asp.radford.edu/Psyc%20405/serial_killer_timelines.htm

Elyria Ohio Chronicle Telegram 09/20/1983

Mind Hunter by John Douglas and Mark Olshaker Pocket Books Copyright 1995

The Most Dangerous Game by Richard Connell, originally published by Collier's Weekly 01/19/24

Butcher Baker by Walter Gilmour and Leland Hale Onyx True Crime Copyright 1991

www.ingramcontent.com/pod-product-compliance
Lightning Source LLC
Chambersburg PA
CBHW020302030426
42336CB00010B/874